CAMPING

ON THE

WYE

WHITNEY

CHEPSTOW.

Four Victorian gents
row the Wye in a
randan skiff in 1892

At Symonds Yat.

ADLARD COLES NAUTICAL

BLOOMSBURY
LONDON · OXFORD · NEW YORK · NEW DELHI · SYDNEY

Adlard Coles Nautical
An imprint of Bloomsbury Publishing Plc

50 Bedford Square   1385 Broadway
London   New York
WC1B 3DP   NY 10018
UK   USA

www.bloomsbury.com
www.adlardcoles.com

ADLARD COLES, ADLARD COLES NAUTICAL and the Buoy logo
are trademarks of Bloomsbury Publishing Plc

First published 2017

British Library Cataloguing-in-Publication Data
A catalogue record for this book is available from the British Library.

Library of Congress Cataloguing-in-Publication data has been applied for.

ISBN: HB: 978-1-4729-4518-1
        ePDF: 978-1-4729-4517-4
        ePub: 978-1-4729-4511-2

2 4 6 8 10 9 7 5 3 1

Typeset in Bembo
Design by Nicola Liddiard, Nimbus Design
Printed in China by C&C Offset Printing Co., Ltd

Preface

This volume, *Camping on the Wye*, together with its sister volume, *A Week on the Broads*, were family treasures handed down to me by my late father, (E.G.L.G. in the narrative). Leather-bound, handwritten and with copious watercolour illustrations on stiff cartridge paper. After many years of handling there is a tendency for the binding to give way, and in the case of the Wye volume my father, being an eminently practical doctor and surgeon, had repaired it with Elastoplast, a favourite material at that time for dressing wounds and sprains, and in its use he was a master craftsman

It was due to my wife Cate and other friends who said the books deserved a wider showing, that I have sought a publisher, and I must thank my sailing friend Tom Dehn and particularly his wife Lorraine for putting me in touch with Bloomsbury Publishing and to Lisa Thomas of Bloomsbury who has guided the actual production from manuscript to publication.

Two other people had a big hand in *Camping on the Wye*, and it happened when I fell into an antiquarian and rare volume bookshop in Ross and Wye owned and run by Philip Tredder. As one does, I mentioned that I had a book in manuscript form with glorious watercolour illustrations, about a descent of the Wye by four students in 1892. On exchanging names, he said, 'Goffe, I only know one other of that spelling and that is my wife's sister who is married to a schoolmaster in south London.' 'You are referring to my nephew Martin I presume,' was my reply. Out of such coincidences was born a collaboration, very one-sided in this case, as it was his wife Sarah, now unfortunately no longer with us, who did the donkey-work transcribing the text into a more legible form. These then are the people I wish to thank for giving this volume the airing that it so richly deserves.

Michael Goffe

Introduction

I have the original sketchbook and handwritten journal of *Camping on the Wye*, together with its companion volume *A Week on the Broads* given to me by my late father, E.G.L.G. or Goffe of the text. He was the last survivor of a group of four students from University College London, who were up for adventures in their long vacation. The title *Camping on the Wye* does not best convey the theme of the book, which describes a descent of a major part of the River Wye in a rowing boat in the year 1892. A more descriptive title might be 'Four Men in a Boat on the Wye' except for the existence of the legendary *Three Men in a Boat* by Jerome K. Jerome about a week on the Thames in a similar boat, and it would be a pity to have any suggestion of plagiarism.

Of the four taking part in the adventure featured in this book, the first, and the one whom I naturally know most about, is my father Ernest George Leopold Goffe – yes my father, not my grandfather – as most people presume. He was born in Port Maria Jamaica in 1867, the ninth son of a well-to-do member of the 'plantocracy', owner of several estates – growing initially sugar, latterly bananas and other crops – a Justice of the Peace and Church Warden. It is a family fable that he was descended from one Willy Goffe, one of Oliver Cromwell's Major Generals who, having signed the death warrant of King Charles I, fled England for North America where he was hunted down by the Redcoats but evaded them with the help of the local settlers. There the trail runs cold until a John Beecham Goffe emerges as a young man with thrust and energy in Jamaica and makes his fortune by buying up bankrupt sugar plantations out of Chancery, and converting them to profitable businesses, as well as by marrying the natural daughter of a well to do member of the plantocracy.

His wife Margaret, so the story goes, was the result of the union between a landowner and his favourite household slave, a reputed beauty. Margaret is listed on her baptismal certificate as a mullato and was brought up and educated within the household and not relegated to the servants' quarters. After marriage they had eleven children, ten boys and one girl, my father being the ninth. As the family estates were given to and managed by the elder brothers, my father was sent to England to study medicine at University College London, in Gower Street, followed by clinical study at University College Hospital. After qualifying, he worked as a hospital doctor at various London hospitals until his marriage to my mother, another doctor, in 1916, when he bought a medical practice in Kingston upon Thames. He worked there for the rest of his career, a much loved and respected GP and surgeon, retiring at the age of 80 in 1948.

During his time at University College and Hospital, he was a member of a group of like-minded young men, keen on sport and adventure which involved beer and girls, little different from today's undergraduates. Of the four taking part, Charles Goring, 'C.G.' of the text, became a doctor who specialised in mental health and criminology and sadly died in 1919 in the post-war influenza epidemic. He was the father of two boys who became my father's wards. The elder, Donald Goring, was killed in a flying accident in Egypt while working for Shell. The younger, Marius Goring became an actor of renown, especially in the classical field and later in television. Both were frequent visitors to our home on Kingston Hill, spending Christmas and other times with us. Their visits were greatly looked forward to by my two elder brothers and I as being older they were able to tell of the exciting life outside home and school.

A. Hair is a complete mystery to me, I cannot remember his name ever being mentioned by my parents, which is surprising as they kept up with a lot of friends from the time before they became so deeply involved in the running of a medical practice and raising a family. He seems in some ways to have been the instigator of the trip and undertaken much of the organisation as well as acting as treasurer to the party and photographer.

S. K. Baker, the author and illustrator of this book and its companion volume *A Week on the Broads* was retired and living on his own when I was introduced to him by my father in 1934. He was deeply shocked that I, at the age of eleven had not heard of or read any of Arthur Ransome's books about the Walker family and their sailing exploits. He gave me his copy of *We Didn't Mean to go to Sea* which I still have and is still my favourite of the series. I am not certain, but I have the idea that he had worked as a civil servant in an office in Whitehall.

The randan skiff that they used on their journey was a typical Thames skiff with three rowing positions which could be used with various combinations of oars, Typically, a single oar for bow and stroke position, a pair of sculls for the midship position or any combination of the three. If idleness was the theme of the day, one person with the pair of sculls from any convenient position could keep the craft moving well while the rest took their ease. At the end of the nineteenth century and the first half of the twentieth century, skiffs of various sizes with one, two or three rowing positions, dinghies, and punts, abounded on the Thames and other navigable rivers and were let out by the day, the week, or longer, and became a popular pastime amongst all classes of society.

In the late nineteenth century the dense network of railway lines spanning the country made boating days out to different places easy. It is of note that our four did not choose a camping skiff, that is one with several metal hoops running from gunwale to gunwale, and supporting an all-enveloping canvas camping cover to provide protection to keep out the rain, give privacy and room to sleep (and, incidentally the downfall of many a maiden as happened to the heroine in A. P. Herbert's, *The Water Gypsies*). Before the days of motorcars and boat-carrying trailers, sending a boat by train was quite the normal thing.

In 1937 my father went to the London Motor Show to buy a new car, and came back having bought a 14ft sailing and rowing dinghy with an outboard engine for less than £50, and this was delivered by train and finally lorry from lee on Sea in Essex to a boatyard in Kingston. The following year, our summer holiday being in Salcombe, with a friend, I loaded the dinghy on to a Southern Railway four-wheeled hand cart and pushed it half a mile through the streets of Kingston to the railway goods yard where it was loaded on to a railway truck and magically delivered to Kingsbridge Station at the head of the Salcombe Estuary. The return journey, three weeks later was nearly as simple except it was an uphill push to the station. I am sorry to say that our progress through the streets was rather mundane and not as colourful as that described in this volume.

The Wye is to this day a largely unspoilt river winding past hills and lovely countryside and only partially tamed with little commercial traffic and still the haunt of salmon and salmon fishers. I have seen no skiffs but many canoes, and there are several boat hirers who will take one up river with a canoe as far as you wish and leave you to travel down at the leisurely pace that the river demands, as rushing down would mean missing seeing the beauty of the surroundings and wildlife. There are occasional rapids which, as long as the river is not in flood, add interest to the journey. I would advise that the lower tidal section is not for the inexperienced but it is still a delightful journey to follow our four in this volume and make a descent of the Wye, for a complete change from the day-to-day stresses of modern life.

The Wye Tour

It wasn't until the middle of the eighteenth century that tourism in the British Isles became an acceptable form of relaxation and a new interest for the gentry. Antiquarians such as William Stukeley not only established a sense of history within the landscape, but also brought a realisation of the potential that buildings and ruins could have in becoming constituent parts of an idealised romantic landscape. The appreciation of such landscapes 'in the raw' led to the 'tours' such as those in the Lake District, the Derbyshire Dales, and the Wye Valley becoming an acceptable alternative to 'taking the waters' at the growing spa towns. The early tourists saw their voyages down the Wye as a sequence of scenic delights that included ruins such as Goodrich Castle and Tintern Abbey. They also saw beauty in the industrial developments in the form of the smoking iron furnaces that littered the riverside, the busy scenes of river traffic, and the commercial activities on the banks. The visual interest in such a tour is well described in the following:

Immediately after passing under Wilton Bridge, we make acquaintance with the peculiarities of the Wye. Its 'winding bounds' are so remarkable that frequently after the boat has floated four or five miles we find ourselves within gun-shot of the place from which we started; a tree-dad hill, or a church-spire, seen directly in front, presently appearing at the side, or, in another moment, behind the spectator; while perhaps in a few minutes, it is immediately again in his onwards path: forming alternately a foreground or a background to the picture, and that so suddenly as to seem incomprehensible. On quitting the level land, the varied and broken scenery on either side suggests a vague though irresistible impression, that the craggy precipices, rocky ascents, and isolated plateaux, between which the stream takes its tortuous way now reposing in deep and glassy pools, then hurrying down a gushing rapid, as if 'behind time', and again stopping to take up at intervals the winding streamlets poured from receding elevations over the little greensward vales they encircle were the boundaries of a river always, in a word, that the Wye is a river designed by Nature itself.

The book of South Wales, the UJYe and the Coast,
Mr. & Mrs. S.C. Hall, 1861

Camping down the Wye, 1892

'A cooling plunge at the break of day,

A paddle, as now on sail;

With always a fish for a midday dish,

And plenty of Adam's ale;

With rod or gun, or in hammock slung,

We glide through the pleasant days:

When darkness falls on our canvas walls,

We kindle the camp fires blaze.'

Edgar

Plinlimmon, the mother of the river Wye, abounding in bogs and morasses, frequently shrouded in mists, and 2469 feet high sends forth from her springs and wells many a noble stream, foremost of which is the Severn, the Wye (150 miles long), the Rheidol, the Dulas etc. A notorious Welsh chieftain, named Owain Glyndwr made it his lair, and from its recesses descended on his forays to the Welsh Marches. At Rhayader the Wye loses its character of an impetuous mountain stream and becomes river-like with occasional shallows. In wet seasons it is navigable at Glasbury, fortunately for us the river of 1892 was a dry one, in fact was lower than for many years and our boat was launched at Whitney, a small village boasting of a railway station about 50 miles from the source. Every part is attractive and the constant windings give ever-changing views, becoming bolder and bolder as it nears its termination. Earthworks of Roman and British origin, stones and crosses, castles and churches abound in the neighbourhood. Salmon and the usual kind of fish are plentiful. The speed of the current is about 5½ miles an hour and the stream is about 10 feet below the alluvial surface. Otter hunting is still carried on in the more remote tributaries. Geologists find the Silurian and Old Red Sandstone, inside some deposits of the Tertiary Period, and affirm that the river has been travelling through its rocky boundaries for no less than 1,2 74,000 years. Very ancient remains of the mammoth, cave bear, rhinoceros and human skeletons have been found in caves, notably those found at Little Doward. In Charles II's reign a sum of £1,300 was raised for the purpose of making the river navigable, traces of the work done may be seen at Mannington Weir etc. Some utilitarian soul proposed to supply London with Wye water to the amount of 393,000,000 gallons per day.

The reader may now wish to be introduced to our little party. It consisted of A. Hair – devoted to salmon fishing and photography, E.G.L.G. – an invaluable man on a camping trip, e.G. – of a philosophic turn of mind, and S.K.B. – a dabbler in art [often recorded as H. Gg., G. and B. in the following account]. It was H. who gathered to himself his friends, and armed with sundry guide books propounded unto them his views on a river camping trip. Jordan, boat builder of Hereford, supplied a Salter's Randan, and after much labour a bell tent was secured and duly pitched in H.'s garden, its divided pole being admirably adapted for packing on board. Two rugs, waterproof sheets, tinned plates, mugs etc. and kit bags were indicated for each man, and a spirit cooking stove for three persons was secured. Groceries with the inevitable tinned meat were ordered to be ready at Paddington, not without protest from G. who had been living on canned provisions for a week on the Broads. Behold then a growler laden with tent, bundle of rugs, kit bags, three Gladstones and H. and Gg. inside descending Haverstock Hill to meet 'G. and B. at the station on the evening of 12 August 1892.

Meeting at Hair's place to discuss ways and means. H. in chair, crammed with guide books etc.

Descent of Haverstock Hill.

A.H.   G.   EKB.   G.L.G.

Meeting at Hair's place to discuss ways and means.
His chair, armed with guide books etc

Descent of Haverstock Hill

Arrival of B.
minus baggage.

Paddington

View of Salter's Randan
at Whitney and a few things
to go into it.

3

Hair's bedroom Hereford
asking for settlement of preliminary Expenses

Luggage having gone wrong we elephant
Hereford : last use of chairs .
Luggage turns up next day and
we form a

B. somehow was late and left his luggage behind, came accompanied however by his banjo and a few spare hats. At Gloucester more luggage got astray and had to be wired for in several directions. We went on to Hereford and were duly met by Jordan. We secured beds and went through a settling of accounts in H.'s bedroom.

Paddington. Arrival of B. minus luggage.

View of Salter's Randan at Whitney and a few things to go into it.

Hair's bedroom, Hereford, asking for settlement
of preliminary expenses.

Luggage having gone wrong in Hereford, last use
of chairs. Luggage turns up next day and we form a ...

Procession through
Hereford.

Photography at
Barr's court station

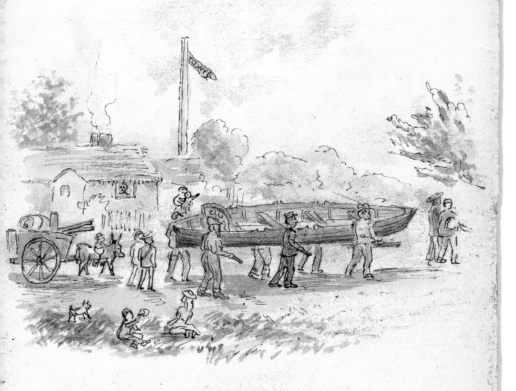

Procession to the River ————————

   1. Joffe and Baker. with banjo
   2. Two platelayers.
   3. Porter & farm hand
   4. platelayers
   5. Hair (with camera) and Goring.
   6. Boy and donkey cart with goods & chattels —

Cottages, children, dogs. etc. etc.

Going down to the river in the morning we found two anxious looking gentlemen seated in an old boat waiting arrival of their canoes. Morning was spent visiting the Cathedral, buying stores and meeting trains for tidings of baggage, this eventually turning up we decided on losing no time in getting on to Whitney. Two porters conveyed our luggage across the city to another station, where we found the boat duly packed on a couple of trucks, our luggage filling a van and after some useful hints from Jordan we arrived in due course at Whitney. The train was somewhat delayed while our ample goods and chattels were deposited on the platform, a passenger throwing us an empty match box, no doubt thinking we had forgotten that useful item.

Procession through Hereford.

Photography at Barr's Court Station.

All the able bodied men in the village came round to assist in conveying us to the river and an imposing procession took place: G. in college blazer and B. with banjo, in the van, next the boat born on poles by men, then a cart with our baggage, H. & G. bringing up the rear. H. distributed ample largesse, and the boat gradually sank with our packing until it rested on the bottom, and much heaving was necessary to get her off.

The procession to the River

1. Goffe and Baker with banjo

2. Two platelayers

3. Porter & farm hand

4. Platelayers

5. Hair (with camera) & Goring

6. Boy and donkey cart with goods

Cottagers, children, dogs, etc., etc.

'A paving porters. Whitney

Loading up.

Our first shoal; all hands overboard,   water
about 4 inches deep

H. Paying porters, Whitney.

We had not rowed far when we grounded again, a contingency provided for by the rule that each man was to jump out and either push or lift the boat.

Loading up,

Our first shoal: all hands overboard, water about 4 inches deep.

Camp at Whitney.

6

Stormy night at
Whitney
Cows and horses
tearing round
the picketed
during night

Enter B.

All snug —

After a mile or so we decided to camp and an elegant site was found nicely sheltered by the trees of a small copse. Unloading proceeded apace, the tent when put up attracting all the cows and horses in the field, water proofs were spread out and bags and baskets lugged inside, and we sat or laid down to await the boiling of the kettle.

Camp at Whitney.

When night fell gusts of wind and rain shook our habitation, necessitating extra stays on the pole, and we lay quaking far into the night, as the animals were charging madly all about us, and at any time we might have entertained a stalled ox and hatred therewith. To those who know not the pleasure of early rising, and there are a good many, a camping trip is to be commended. You wake and feel that you are truly one with nature. After that blissful half awake state succeeding a dreamless sleep, you throw off rugs and clad in flannels emerge directly into the sweet morning air warmed by the sun and laden with the promise of a lovely day. The grass stalks laden with dew, gently stirred by passing zephyrs love your feet, the birds welcome you, the smoke and endless turmoil of the town is as a forgotten dream. With towels swinging you make for the bathing place and take an invigorating header into the pure cool water. The odour of frying bacon and eggs is then doubly grateful and the coffee delicious, boiling on a fire made of wood from the copse. Foaming fresh milk in abundance and marmalade wherewith to fill the crevices complete the meal. All sit round to discuss the morning pipe and plans for the day. Of course there are certain disagreeables, for instance when H. resignedly disappears with the crockery down to the water's edge and dabbles about in the mud to clear off the grease, we know as we sit and smoke that perhaps he does not take everything as cheerfully as he might. This general disinclination to 'wash up' may account for the gradual merging of one meal into the rest. A shop in the village was found where bread, apples and oil were sold and we added a goodly supply to our store.

Stormy night at Whitney. Cows and horses tearing around the field during night.

Enter B.

All snug.

Afternoon callers.   The vicar invites us to Church and
                        to tea at the Vicarage.

The transit
of Venus!

& Eclipse by the
    Sun-shade.

" The shades of night were falling fast —
And H's pot did boil at last "

" He lay like a warrior taking his rest,
With his Y.M.S.C cloak around him " G. asleep.

We discovered that we were near a path, and that the path led to a house, from which house strolled the owner with not exactly an expression of welcome on his face. H. & G. who were in charge at the time artlessly tried weather topics and other things, but when the gentleman caught sight of G. & B. down the river, fishing, he mildly suggested that we 'might have asked leave'. However, satisfactory explanations ensued and later on he returned accompanied by a clergyman who, to the honour of his cloth, invited us to church and tea. Now, some of us on a visit to the village had given heed unto the gossip of the place relating how a tent exactly like ours had been torn to pieces by cows, the owners perforce having to return to town sooner than they expected and as it had been established that where 'one of us went the others went too', we laid our bodily necessities before our spiritual and decided to stay in camp, thereby missing much that was delightful; for G. et B. strolling round the church in the evening saw a lovely vision of a fair damsel who was ascertained to be the vicar's daughter!

Afternoon callers. The Vicar invites us to Church and tea at the Vicarage.

The transit of Venus.

Eclipse by the sun-shade

Tea over, the strangeness of the thing came over us, but G. who has camped much (with the Volunteer Medical Service Corps) after a survey of the heavens disappeared with a spade and dug a trench all round. We disposed ourselves for sleep, two of the crew first warbling a few duets until G.'s snores drowned all else.

'The shades of night were falling fast – and H.'s pot did boil at last'

'He lay like a warrior taking his rest." G. asleep with his T.M.S.C cloak around him.

Allarums and Excursion

Warrior and Excursion.

Bathe before breakfast at Whitney.
Instantaneous Photography.

Bathe before breakfast at Whitney. Instantaneous photography.

G. offe disturbed in the early morning by bovine
and equine curiosity discharges the deadly
air gun at the intruders: a tiny thud shews
that he has hit something it is followed by
a lumbering trot and a general want of
further interest on the part of the animals -
However cows brought their calves to see us
later on with pardonable feminine curiosity

Furnace bursts at **Whitney**.
" *Rocks, plates & pans confus'ly hurled* "

Ye small boy seeketh to inspire Terror by ye Tale of ye Mad Bulle.

Early morn proved that G. sleeps with one eye open for seizing his air gun he rushed out and fired several times into a crowd of bovine visitors that were jostling each other to get inside the tent. A tiny thud, showing that he has hit something, is followed by a lumbering trot and a general want of interest on the part of the animals. However, cows brought their calves to see us later on with pardonable feminine curiosity.

This roused us all and 'getting up' was suggested but nobody stirred until B. found some beetles under his rug and got up without further ado. Soon four men variously attired were engaged in spreading rugs out to air, breakfast was set in order, and, presently at a word from H. who had his camera ready, the others dived into the water from the boat with a mighty splash. Unfortunately this interesting scene, like one or two others of great interest didn't 'develop' as H. had forgotten his 'shutter'.

Goffe disturbed in the early morning by bovine and equine curiosity discharges the deadly air gun at the intruders; a tiny thud shows that he has hit something it is followed by a lumbering trot and a general wont of further interest on the part of the animals. However cows brought their calves to see us later on with pardonable feminine curiosity.

Furnace bursts at Whitney. "Rocks, plates and pans confus'ly tumbled.

Ye small boy seeketh to inspire Terror by ye Tale of Ye Mad Bulle.

Men working on bank direct us as to
negociating first rapid.

Men working on bank direct us as to negotiating first rapids.

Evening at Mannington Camp.

Evening at Mannington Camp.

These two somewhat inebriated looking gentlemen
are really tinkering up a hole in the boat.

The Fall at Monnington.

Bare legged we brought ashore a most
tempting lunch from the boat, there was
pine apple, beer, bloater paste, onions. bread
a table cloth, cheese, plates two Knives
and a fork. Let those laugh who may.
but men requires sustenance such as this
for the arduous labours of Wye navigation
Without food who could endure the
many hardships and perils of the river?

These two somewhat inebriated gentlemen are really tinkering
up a hole in the boat.

The fall at Monnington.

Bare legged we brought ashore a most tempting lunch from the boat, there was a pineapple, beer, bloater paste, onions, bread, a table cloth, cheese, plates, two knives and a fork. Let those laugh who may but men require sustenance such as this for the arduous labours of Wye navigation. Without food who could endure the many hardships and perils of the river.

Nasty Snags.

A well earned repast.

Easy all!

Here Going doeth no small deed of daring, and rescues
two damsels in distress

On Monday morning we struck tent and dropped down the hurrying river. Shallows bothered us somewhat at first and also the rapids, but by steering for the tongue of smooth water at the head of each fall we generally got through alright. Our feet and legs became sunburnt with exposure as we wore trousers turned up so as to be ready for emergencies. Sometimes the current would almost tear the boat out of our hands and when the others had got in the indefatigable G. would be hanging on desperately to the stern, then with a tremendous leap land on the top of bags, hats and general cargo, when the boat would plunge ahead, water seething all around and the stones at the bottom appearing to fly past. We stationed a man at the bow to fend her off going round corners as she had a nasty way of burying her nose in the bank, and his work was no sinecure as the bent pole often testified. At very awkward channels all got out and hung on until the best course was decided on. Occasionally jagged boulders would be seen, so close as to cause a shudder, and sometimes after a long scrunch we would 'get left' on the top of another, deep water all around into which G. once or twice boldly plunged, a veritable Jonah; a jab here and there usually sufficient to keep her right. Now comes a murmuring shoal right across the river and the good old boat would scrape along in a half-hearted manner.

Nasty snags.

A well-earned repast

*Then comes a long quick reach, perhaps a leaping salmon alone breaking
its placid surface. Just the place for lunch-and stroke dives into basket after
bread and cheese. Lolling on seats and baggage all take a rest while the
soothing weed sends up tiny cloudlets to join those above ... too soon
another rapid demands attention, (the general impression on nearing a
rapid is that it is approaching us like some great river dragon, whereas it
is we who are being borne rapidly by the stream into the midst of rushing
shallows), or perhaps the guide book says something of interest is to be
seen and we land to investigate. Afloat once more song resounds far
down the stream, H. giving a verse of the Canadian boat song:*

Faintly as tolls the evening chime,

Our voices keep tune and our oars keep time

Soon as the words on the shore look dim

We'll sing of St. Anne's own parting hymn –

Row, brothers, row the stream runs fast

The rapids are near and the daylight's past

Easy all!

Here Goring doeth no small deed of daring and rescues two
damsels in distress.

Fishing. Crabs.

That ardent piscator. H

waging war on the finney tribe

doth greatly disturb the equilibrium

of our craft

Snags and Shallows
at Bredwardine.

We land at an Inn, where G. obliges with the
" Polka and the choir Boy " Harmonium accompt.
      Lunch. We involuntarily present the
people with our beer jar

Expletives
G. "gets left"

Now does Gg. try to secure game for the larder by shooting at rabbits which of course clear into holes on seeing the bullet, and now H. walks about in the boat casting the fly all round, 'though never a fish comes out to dine', whilst greatly disturbing the equilibrium of our craft.

Gg. disgusted at rabbits seeks refuge in some mighty tome, while the jovial G. describes himself as a 'simple country maiden with a beauty heavy laden', or launching out into piratical sentiments sings out that 'once aboard the lugger the girl is mine, and then?' 'Ah! Ah!' roar the crew in chorus, sending some flapping heron miles down the river miles down the river in disgust.

At Bredwardine a former student of the U.C.H. has set up for himself a practice and a landing party is formed of G. & B., the latter somewhat inconvenienced by a flapping rubber sole. However the place is under repair and the deputation withdraws, and find H. & G. eating apples in an orchard. G. is presented with a button hole of daisies by little girls at the toll gate and they demand the rest of 1d. each.

Fishing. Crabs. That ardent piscator H. waging war on the turning tide doth greatly disturb the equilibrium of our craft.

Snags and shallows at Bredwardine.

We land at an Inn, where G obliges with the "polka and Choir Boy". Harmonium accompt Lunch.

We understandably present these people with our beer jar.

Expletives. G "gets left".

Children Scrambling for cuttapus

Boy having found one, stands by it, for little girl to pick up. So now we see a bald chanticleer lay bare some choice morsel for the hens of his choice to eat.

S. "Once aboard the lugger, the gurl is mine, and then?"

Chorus. f.f. ah-ah!

14

A dewy eve
at Monk's Boat
House near Henford

Each has his allotted task —
Sawing makes a furnace in the bank, H. lugs things.
Saffe with never-to-be-sufficiently-admired skill pitches
the Tent. B. tears down half a tree. The owner
looks on.

"Stick to them G."! He does, and provides the
camp with fresh water from other side the River.
Good old G.

Easy all!

Once more we board the lugger, and soon a mighty fall is heard. We drift down cautiously and find a singular bed of flat sandstone rocks covering three fourths of the river, which confined on the left rushes through a narrow channel roaring over great boulders on either side.

This is rather a serious check and we pitch tent in a leafy dell facing the fall at sunset; a forage party visits a neighbouring farm for apples & milk; while G. climbs a tree the farmer's wife and B. receive the fruit. Heavy laden they return, a furnace having meanwhile been made in the bank. Lulled to sleep by the fall, snores resound from the tired voyagers.

Children scrambling for coppers. A boy having found one, stands by it, for the little girl to pick up. So noone sees bold chanticleer lay bare some choice morsel for the hens of his choices to eat.

G. "Once aboard the lugger, the girl is mine, and then?"

Chorus of 'Ah! Ah'!

Morning, with the song of birds, finds us ready for breakfast but somewhat subdued by Gg. pointing out a decayed hedgehog floating in the pool from which he had drawn water over-night. Now G. & B. betake them to the boat which had got a nasty knock the previous day, and finding a hole, rivet a strip of cedar over it. The luggage having been carried over the portage, the boat is towed round, held by a line from the stern to prevent her being drawn into the current. After hauling over rocks she takes the water below, and cargo being stowed we let go and quickly leave the fall. G. was with difficulty dissuaded from plunging through the fearful channel – fatal accidents had happened there, and we could not afford to loose our G.! The sun was high in the heavens when lunch was proposed, and carried up the bank to a flowery mead. A waterproof served for a tablecloth, and the river received a choice collection of empty tins and pots.

Evening found us at the Monk's Boat House but seeing a ghostly advisor strolling round we decided on pitching on the opposite bank, so perpendicular as to necessitate hauling things up by ropes.

'Here today and gone tomorrow?' remarked a woman passing in a boat. The welcome stew from Gg.'s pot put warmth into our souls and the duplex lamp the same thing for the tent. We lay around smoking and imbibing ale until one after another we fell asleep.

A dewy camp at Monk's Boat house near Hereford. Each has his allotted task – Goring makes a furnace in the bank, H. lugs things, Goffe with never-to-be-sufficiently-admired skill pitches the tent. B. tears down half a tree. The owner looks on.

'Stick to it G!' He does, and provides the camp with fresh water from the other side of the river. Good old G.

Awful Discovery!

Trials of the Amateur Photographer.!

& Affair finds after about 40 "Snaps"
that he has forgotten to have the Shutter up.

15

Otter, supposed to have been seen by B.
(since discovered that theabove was cribbed
from a picture by Landseer.)

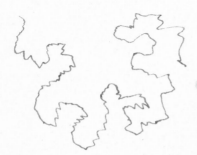

Zig-gagerated view of the Wye.
man in boat — Can't get over, can you?
No, shall have to go round,
its only a few miles

Awful discovery! Trials of the amateur photographer. Hair finds
after about 40 "Snaps" that he has forgotten to have the shutter up.

Otter, supposed to have been seen by B. I since discovered that the above was cribbed from a picture by Landseer.

Zig-gagerated view of the Wye. Man on boat – Can't get over, can you? No, shall have to go round, it's only a few miles.

Pisgah.

Hereford from the River. Photo by H.

The middle arch of this bridge was
destroyed by Cromwells, since
restored

Pisgah.

Next day saw us at Hereford and we landed for stores and some baggage which had arrived from London, changing oars for a pair of sculls, and purchasing river charts. Gg. and B. arrived from the market with arms and pockets laden and with welcome letters from the P.O. No time was lost in getting off and the Cathedral towers soon faded into the distance. More shoals and rapids, and the sculls began to show signs of wear for the turns were frequent and much poling necessary.

Hereford from the River, photo by H. The middle arch of the bridge was destroyed by Cromwell, since restored.

Going & B foraging for provisions at Hereford, not
forgetting bunting (U. K. colours)

Ancient Briton going fishing in his Coracle.

17

Camp of Canoeists at Casey Woods.

Nice evening, isn't it.

Very, going down?

Well, yes. Staying here long?

Tomorrow, see you again.

Yes. ta. ta.

Ta. ta.

Goring and B. foraging for provisions at Hereford, not forgetting bunting (U.C.H. colours)

Ancient Briton going fishing in his coracle.

A lovely reach with banks crowned with trees, cattle standing knee deep in the stream watching us with 'slow bovine gaze' lashing each other's sides with tails, close packed the better to keep off flies, brought us to a lofty tree covered hill. At the angle of the river appeared a balloon tent, occupants seated outside with liquids on a table, smoking cigarettes, canoes hauled up on land. We hailed them and recognised canoeists from Hereford, having been about a week on that part of the journey.

Dropping down we pulled up at a field — real steps in the bank the better to unload, borrowing hedge stakes to support our pots and kettle over the fire. Now, supper being finished and all men weary the others slept while Gg. discoursed on philosophy, a stillness settled down over all things, a lurid light filled the tent, and some creature gave a sharp cry, the earth trembled and the watchers felt thankful that they slept not in houses as do most men but in a tent. Then pipes giving out they also went to sleep and in the morning spoke of these things to the others who thereupon laughed them to scorn. Canoeists passing said they had felt nothing but a few beetles during the night. An unromantic shepherd hammered on our tent and seemed aggrieved at the use of his poles.

Camp of canoeists at Carey Woods.

'Nice evening, isn't it.'

'Very, going down?' 'Well, yes. Staying here long?'

'Tomorrow. See you again.' 'Yes, ta ta.' 'Ta, ta.'

G. and B. discussing last pipe and
philosophy in a mystic luminous light
at Carey woods. Suddenly hear strange cry
of bird followed by a tremor of the earth,
a "slight seismic disturbance" as G.
puts it; the others absolutely sceptical
in morning of course.

Just because
we had used a
few miserable
hedge-stakes
for our fire
overnight an
irate shepherd
comes round in
the morning and
makes row. Saffe,
half asleep, in reply to his remonstrances
says we don't require steaks, but would
be glad to know where milk can be
obtained.

Exit shepherd, grumbling—
N.B. It is but fair to ourselves to say
that we did as little damage as possible,
and always paid our way. the stakes here
mentioned were duly stuck in the same holes
(or thereabouts) on leaving camp.

G. and B. discussing last pipe and philosophy in a mystic luminous light at Carey Woods, suddenly near strangery of bird followed by a tremor of the Earth, a "slight seismic disturbance" as G. puts it: the others absolutely sceptical in morning of course.

Just because we had used a few miserable hedge-stakes for our fire overnight an irate shepherd comes round in the morning and makes row. Goffe, half asleep, in reply to his remonstrances says we don't require steaks, but would be glad to know where milk can be obtained.

Exit shepherd grumbling – NB. It is but fair to ourselves to say that we did as little damage as possible and always paid our way. The stakes hero mentioned was duly stuck in the same hall (or thereabouts) on leaving camp.

Discussion!
as to how long water-proofs are
worthy of the name. Compulsory
trial of an hour or so.
" O. why left I my name?"
And we are down the wrong channel
but half an hour's pull in the rain
puts that all right. and everybody
blames every-body else for taking us wrong

We run into some rocks above Foy.
fortunately, no damage done. It
is difficult to know when to go
generally and while you are thinking
about it you find the boat going
broadside   on at the rate of ten
miles an hour on to   stones,
or, as in this case, bear on to the
bank, the current then whirling you
are over the river.

Loading up we cleared off after breakfast and arrived in the rain in some cui de sac. Donning macs we pulled under some trees and waited for that rain to stop. A discussion ensued as to how long water-proofs are worthy of the name, with a compulsory trial of an hour or so. Then we find we are down the wrong channel, but half an hour's pull in the rain puts that right, and everybody blames everybody else for taking us the wrong way. It cleared at last and getting into the proper channel we arrived at a farm where flat rocks suggested a bathe. G. suggested leapfrog and deluged us with water as his mighty form disappeared in the foaming wave. B. took a walk of several miles and the boat, relieved of his 12 stone, speeded cheerily on. Grand views of the winding stream appeared through the trees, the boat like an energetic beetle far down below.

Discussion as to how long waterproofs are worthy of the name. Compulsory trial of an hour or so.

"Oh why left I my name?"

Find we are down the wrong channel but half an hour's pull in the rain puts that all right and everybody blames everybody else for taking no money.

Later on a sharp turn and swift current wedged the boat's nose in some stones in the bank, she swung round to flee down stream stern first – a lucky escape.

We ran into some rocks above Foy. Fortunately no damage done. It is dificult to know where to go generally and while you are thinking about it you find the bank going broadside on at the rate of ten miles an hour onto stones or, as in this case, bow onto the bank: the current then whirling you all over the river.

On Foy Island.

Encampment at Foy. For fishing H. says this
beat anything he had seen so far. and comes
in with some superb salmon about 1/2 oz.
in weight.   eaten   for breakfast next
morning

Ancient horsekeeper
calls and lingers
while yet the steaming
pots give forth
appetising odours;
declining invitation
to dine, he at length
departs with 1/-. He
had told his missis that he "know't they boys
was up to summat."

The rustic
taste has
not been
Educated
up to
Camp Curry;
however a
boy devoured
remains of
our "Aus" Ram

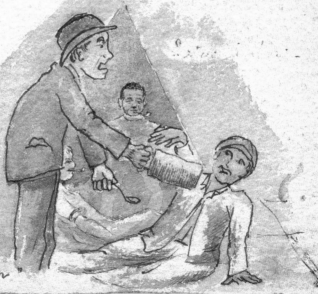

It was yet early times when a tight little island hove in sight, called Foy; we took possession by planting our colours. It was a much bepastured spot, and disturbing horses, cows, ducks and geese we at last found a space for camp.

On Foy Island.

For fishing H says this beat anything he had seen so far, and comes in with some infant salmon, eaten for breakfast the next morning.

The entire occupants of a house came to the door and duly gave permission to camp. Our envoy returning and reporting young women, G. discovered we wanted milk, and accompanied maiden to the roost etc. The contents of the boat having meanwhile been deposited in the mud, H. & Gg. engaged in fishing. A heaving struggling mass of canvas contained G., & B. dug a trench for the fire. Enters an elderly man who did not appear to have seen anything quite so wonderful as our arrangements in all his life. A small gratuity secured us against the horses, and the old man who might have been an ancient Briton retired well pleased. He had told his missis that he they boys was up to summat'. Our piscators returned bearing finny spoil, and supper was indicated. While engaged thereon we heard voices and B. mounted guard with air gun and challenged them. They thereupon came up and derived much edification from a contemplation of our domestic arrangements. G. showed them the deadly nature of the gun on insects of which we had a few, and we handed remains of our curry to a man who after tasting it, smiled sadly, and gave to some boys who got through it safely.

Ancient horsekeeper calls and lingers while yet the steaming pots give forth appetizing odours; declining invitation to dine, he at length departs with 1/-. He had told his missus that he "knowt' they boys was up to summat".

The rustic taste has not been educated up to camp curry; however a boy devoured remains of our 'Aus' Ram.

I was justly proud of his idea for airing things,
and was (very properly) photographed by H.

" But O! what a difference" when the wind blew"

Town Hall. Ross. temp. Charles II.

"Lologram" cut in stone in S. wall of Market House, Ross
supposed to "signify" Faithful to Charles in heart"
and placed there by John Kyrle, The Man of Ross. 1680.

G. was very justly proud of his idea for airing things, and was (very properly) photographed by H.

'But O! What a difference' when the wind blew.

It was dark, but we accepted the man's invite to visit the 'Hole in the Wall', and after floundering through mud and water found a spring. Higher up in the rocks water could be heard trickling. The man's household supplied us with salt for a month. Passing a farmhouse G. saw female shadows on the blind and returned in ecstasy.

The man brought us a bushel of apples in the morning after which we got away and arrived at Ross, surveying the Prospect, calling at the P.O., at the church, the Town Hall and the 'Saracen's Head' (for wood carvings). B. was absurdly proud of a white flannel cap he had purchased, and a fisherman discoursed on salmon fishing.

Ross Town Hall, tomb of Charles II

'Sologram' cut in stone in south wall of market house, Ross, supposed to signify 'Faithful to Charles in heart' and placed there by John Kyrle, The Man of Ross, 1680.

Elms recently growing inside Ross Church.
                              Photo by H.

                    legend relates that
A vicar cut down the Man of Ross's own
particular tree outside the church, whereupon
two young ones sprang up through the floor
and flourished inside the window to the
great delight of the people. The stems
now only remain, but a creeper gives
to one the appearance of life

22

At Fay camp a
man became much
interested in
our message, and
supplied us with pears,
apples, and salt, also
shewing us "The Hole in
the Wall" from which
orifice issued cooling
streams - We struck
camp, and paddled down

until the ruins of, Goodrich Castle came
in sight.

Goodrich castle

Elms growing inside Ross church. Photo by H.

Legend relates that a vicar cut down the Man of Ross's own particular yew outside the church, whereupon two young ones sprang up through the floor and flourished inside the window to the great delight of the people. The stems now only remain, but a creeper gives to one the appearance of life.

At Foy camp a man became much interested in our ménage, and supplied us with pears, apples and salt, also showing us 'The Hole in the Wall' from which drifted mined coalling streams. We struck camp and paddled down until the ruins of Goodrich Castle came in sight.

Goodrich Castle

Goodrich
Castle.

The
Lady's
Tower.

We were delighted to find a fair artist at
work in the central court, giving an opportunity
to G. who is a great art critic to render
valuable assistance. The evening drawing
on she packed up and made her way to
Goodrich Court, which is on the next brow
picturesqly built overlooking the Wye.

23

To Castle

We form a procession with baggage up to the Castle, about 1/4 mile from the River.

Afloat again we passed Wilton Castle on the right, and arrived at Goodrich Castle. A gamekeeper gave us permission to camp, (rather an ambitious project as our luggage was great and the castle up a hill some distance from the river). However a procession was formed but soon collapsed.

Here Gg. was prostrate, stretched like Issachar between two burdens, there B. seated on bundle of rugs mopping his perspiring brow, and then goes G. staggering under three kit bags, and a couple of Gladstones, muttering condemnatory remarks on things in general. H. was occupying himself in getting the thousand and one things out of the boat. Oars and poles were deposited in the undergrowth, and eventually everything was got up to the Castle. The custodian eyed us somewhat askance; he was used to people visiting, but here we were come evidently came to stay. We told him we had permission (without mentioning authority) and he was affability itself.

B. had been here before and asked after the old man's wife, on which he burst into tears, she was 'gone'; she had told B. that 'She was as weak as a robin'. The good old man did not forget to mention as to fees, and promised to come in the morning and bring his fiddle.

Surrounded by ruined walls we pitched our tent, a fine place was found, and soon the roaring fire was boiling soup and cooking proceeded under the able hands of Gg.

Goodrich Castle. The Lady's Tower.

We were delighted to find a fair artist at work in the central court, giving an opportunity to G. who is a great art critic to render valuable assistance. The evening drawing on she packed up and made her way to Goodrich Court, which is on the next bend, picturesquely built overlooking the Wye.

We form a procession with baggage up to the castle, about
a ¼ mile from the River.

Soing— " We are almost done up quite "

More stores for the
Camp.

From photo. by H. This was the best
pitch we had, free from coleoptera, diptera, etc
In the morning the joyous doves, jackdaws
and owls sang their hymn of praise and
then wended their way to their happy hunting
grounds leaving us to our breakfasts and
the enjoyment of a lovely day. No previous
tent has been pitched there since Cromwell
battered at its walls, at which time the
brave defenders on giving in were treated
with all the honours of war.

Goring – "Me am almost done up quite,"

More stores from the camp.

From photo by H. This was the best pitch we had, free from coleoptera, diptera, etc. In the morning the joyous doves, jackdaws and owls sung their hymns of prase and then wended their way to their happy hunting grounds leaving us to our breakfasts and the enjoyment of a lovely day. No previous tent has been pitched there since Cromwell battered at its walls, at which time the more defenders on giving in were treated with all the honours of war.

We dine in the Banqueting Hall (rather eerie)
and though we called on the scullions to
clear up there was no voice. Save the
bleating of sheep or the restless cry of some
birds.

Good old Gig does the cooking and
nearly roasts himself into the bargain
in a very convenient corner of an
old staircase. The draught was so
great that very soon a pile of
sticks put there by somebody was
consumed. The curry formed
the pièce de resistance at the Banquet

We naturally turned to the Banqueting Hall and under a starry roof, on a table made of loose boards, we spread our dish cloth, sorry! tablecloth, and with a lamp at each end the steaming stew did make unto ourselves an unctuous feast.

'Gadzooks' and 'Grammercy' likewise 'ods bobs' and 'byie halidom'! We are in the Middle Ages once again! Were not the shadows on the wall those of long lost heroes? Is not that clanking sound the mailed sentry on the ramparts? 'Nay! twas but the wind Or the tin upsetting on the raging fire On with the feast! Let belts be unconfIned No rest till morn, when tinned Ram we eat.'

We dine in the Banqueting Hall (rather eerie) and though we called on the scullions to clear up, there was no voice, save the bleating of sheep or the restless cry of some bird.

The fine old castle must have looked odd from the village, quite haunted with lights shining through the gaping windows. The rage of hunger now appeased, we sat round and smoked our pipes moralizing on fallen greatness and generally enjoying the reward of our excursions. No sound but the 'night winds whispering low' the ghosts of knights and ladies, the Lords of Goodrich and of that brave garrison which in King Charles' reign held out for five months against Cromwell's Roundheads, passed before us peopling the ruined courts. A chief named Godricus Dux built the castle and King John presented it to William Strigul in 1204. The keep is more ancient and was built by an Irish chieftain as ransom for his son. 'In shape the castle is a parallelogram, with round towers at its angles and is entered by a long passage divided into sections by gates and portcullis'. The visitor of obnoxious intent was received with boiling water in one, molten lead in the next, probably brick bats in another while arrows would rattle on his armour all the way. It is not a matter for surprise therefore that the castle was not entered by the passage but rather the Lady's Tower in the wall of which a huge gap appears.

We made for the tent, and wrapped in our rugs slept peacefully till dawn. The ruins abounded in owls chanting in crescendo, chattering jackdaws and cooing pigeons, which delightful noises ceased gradually as day drew on. Seated on benches (a luxury for us) we breakfasted in the warm sun, H. taking snap shots.

Good old Gg. does the cooking and nearly roasts himself into the bargain in a very convenient corner of an old case. The draught was so great that very soon a pile of sticks put there by somebody was consumed. The curry formed the piece de resistance at the Banquet.

S. obliges with the "pas de quatre" by himself

26

B and G waltz.

" Till they laughing, tumble flat upon the ground ".

Drawings in the Castle attributed to Henry IV.

The tent was struck and the janitor appeared shortly after. B borrowed the fiddle and played the 'pas de quatre', G. dancing and the old man striking up a waltz that became general. The old man's nieces and some girls and some visitors arrived and we scaled the walls, were shown the dungeons, and some freehand drawings by King Henry IV.

G. obliges with the 'pas de quatre' – by himself.

Rolling things down the slopes was easier than carrying them, oars were dragged from their hiding place, the boat loaded and we dropped down the river for a bathe. Refreshed, we rowed on until the gigantic vertical cliffs of Coldwell Rocks appeared, 600 feet high and quite chilly in the shade. Once more we glide into the sunshine.

B. and G. waltz, 'Till they laughing, tumble flat upon the ground'.

Drawings in the Castle attributed to Henry IV.

Incident on another boating trip (Morgan & Baker)

Towing the derelict ashore.

Having got fixed on some rocks, they tried wobbling
to get her off; with the result that several holes were
knocked in the boat, and B. had to swim ashore.

" By the waters of Babylon."
Despair of M and B. To them enter man with
mustard tin, hammer & nails

27

Lunch in Goodrich castle -

photo by A. Hair.

Menu .. probably a stew of some sort .

Incidents on another boating trip: Morgan and Baker.

Towing the derelict ashore.

Having got forced on some rocks, they tried wobbling to get him off; with the result that several holes were knocked in the boat, and B had to swim ashore.

'By the waters of Babylon.' Despair of M. and B. So they entertain with mustard tin, hammer and nails.

Lunch in Goodrich Castle.

Mem. probably a stew of some sort.

RADNOR

HEREFORD

WHITNEY CAMP.

TRETON.
BROBURY.
MONNINGTON. CAMP.
BREDWARDINE.
MOCCAS.

CAMP.
CLEHONGER.

HEREFORD.
CASTLE.

BRECKNOCK

BALLINGHAM.

FOY. CAMP.

ROSS.

CASTLE.
GOODRICH
CAMP.
Little Howard.
DIXTON.

WELSH BICKNOR.

SYMONDS YAT.

MONMOUTH

MONMOUTH.
CASTLE.

Llandogo.

FOREST OF DEAN.

Bigswear.

TINTERN
ABBEY.

CAMP.

WYND
CLIEF
CASTLE.
CHEPSTOW.
CAMP.

Map of the Wye
from Whitney to Chepstow.

at Symonds Yat

Map of the Wye from Whitney to Chepstow.

At the New Weir B. became somewhat pensive, for was it not here that a former trip was cut short by a catastrophe to the boat which filled and sank after running on the rocks. The wreck was sent back on a donkey cart to Ross and the two occupants did a thumb to Chepstow, their destination. The sculls having become damaged B. spliced the blades with wire, and we arrived at the most picturesque part of the river – Symonds Yat (signitying the Gate of the Wye). Our boat aroused the languid interest of the watermen and we left it in their charge to climb the steep cliffs to the top of the Yat, a huge mass of carboniferous limestone. The river may be seen winding in a curve of four miles, while the distance across the Yat is a little under 600 yards. The Welsh Hills, Coldwell Rocks, Forest of Dean and many villages form a splendid panorama.

At Symonds Yat.

Midnight Tea, Dinner & Supper at L Doward.

Cook. log.
I say, you
fellows, bring
out a little
pepper, and
some salt
dont forget
the curry
powder, and

the butter, the potatoes are done, so is the steak.
I am putting on the beans, I am looking aff
"Pudding". Chorus "Oh bother all that. Bring it in
as it is."

29

Dawn at Symonds Yat

H. had left us at Welsh Bicknor, striking across fields for the station to get meat and photo requisites, and seeing a train come in we could see him sigh as he contemplated the climb in store having recognised our handkerchiefs waving away up. G. held a levee of small country maidens laden with ginger-pop, a glorious sunset giving charming tints to the hills around.

Midnight Tea, Dinner and Supper at L. Daward.

Cook. Coq.

I say. You fellows, bring out a little pepper, and some salt and forget the curry powder and the butter, the potatoes are done, so is the steak. I am putting on the beans, I am cooking up 'pudding'. Chorus – 'Oh bother all that. Bring it in as it is.'

Descending, we got afloat and paddled through darkening ravines looking in vain for a suitable camping ground. Deep pools, some 60 feet deep, mark the approach to the Little Doward below which is a dangerous channel through rocks. We crept along slowly in the darkness until the sound of broken water ahead put us very much on the qui vive. Getting the boat's nose pointed for the narrow channel we let her go, and in a moment were through and poling vigorously to keep her from running into the bank. She came through very well considering the darkness. Finding a low bank on the left we stopped the boat and with all haste unloaded. G. got up the tent and a hasty meal was ready at about 10.30pm – a kind of amalgamation as we had had neither lunch, dinner, tea nor supper and now ate enough for all four; retiring soon after we slept well and woke to find the sun shining brilliantly.

Dawn at Symonds Yat.

More Instantaneous photography.
G. requests Gig to tuck in his tuppenny."

Natural History.

The opposite page being rather limited
does not do full justice to the many
beautiful objects in the insect world
that invaded our tent nightly on the
lamp being lit. Here we see G.
doing execution with his air-gun and
Gig fishing out a remarkably fine specimen
of the order Diptera from the jam pot
before beginning his breakfast.

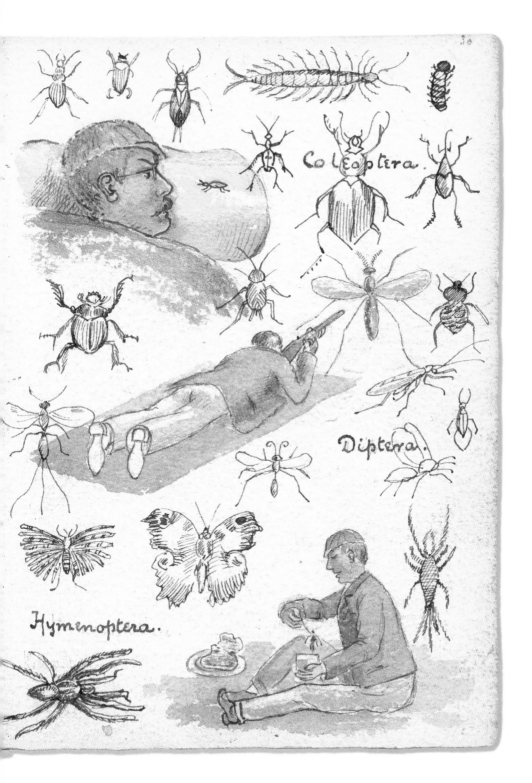

Coleoptera.

Diptera.

Hymenoptera.

A gamekeeper of cheery disposition came to see us, and made us welcome over the adjoining demesne, his master being away from home. He said that some fellows had pitched a tent in the neighbouring woods with intent to live on game, but were starved out.

More instantaneous photographs.

G. requests Gg. to tuck in his tuppeny

Natural history

The opposite pages being rather limited does not do full justice to the many beautiful objects in the insect world that invaded our tent nightly on the lamp being lit. Here we see G. doing execution with his airgun, and Gg. fishing out a remarkably fine specimen of the order Diptera from the jam pot before beginning his breakfast.

Coleoptera

Diptera

Hymenoptera

Monmouth from Little Doward
with Kent and "Slaughter" below.
Scene of sanguinary conflict between
Romans and Britons —
about A.D. 49.

Caractacus on guard. Little Doward.

an ancient British Camp.

He was eventually taken prisoner to Rome, but was pardoned by Claudius.

Later on we crossed the river and after a steep climb found on the far side some caves-Arthur's Cave, Arthur's Hall etc. – exploring same with lantern, but finding no relics of habitation although bones of all kinds had been discovered. Those of red deer, grouse etc. were seen, and we rather ungratefully brought away a hawk's skull as a memento, found tied to a stick as a warning to others.

Monmouth from Little Doward with tent and 'Slaughter' below.

Scene of sanguinary conflict between Romans and Britons about AD 49.

*'Here is a well preserved British Camp, with a double vallum on the N.E.
and a quadrangular area open on the S.E. but otherwise defended by steep
cliffs'* · *This is said to be a camp of Caractacus who from this place bade
defiance to the Roman general, Ostonus, and had such a battle in the
passage that it is called the 'Slaughter' unto this day. A well-like cavity
contained a skeleton of large size and a long excavation of about a mile
was used for exercising horses. A tumulus covers the remains of some long
forgotten hero of whom might be written, as of a similar chieftain's grave
found in Cornwall: What noble dead lies here Lone on this moorland
drear ... Haply is here the grave of Briton warrior brave ... Who deemed
that here might fame to later years proclaim His val'rous deeds:- but
faithless to its trust Fame hath not left the venerated dust The shadow
of a name*

*Ascending a tower of slender iron work with H. below with camera we
had a fine view, and also discovered some tokens left there by a young
couple of amorous feelings. Coming down we struck a path with sundry
boughs strewn across, probably to warn carts etc. of the presence of wire
netting enclosing young pheasants. In the village a travelling bear was
amusing the youngsters. We came across our friend the gamekeeper and
had another chat, and discovered several caverns, selecting the most break
neck routes down to the river.*

Caractacus on guard. Little Doward.

An ancient British camp.

He was eventually taken priosner to Rome, but was pardoned
by Claudius.

Farmer welcomes us and sends for cyder.

A most worthy host, his cousins sisters and aunts
took much interest in our camp life, and
approached the Tent with a view to inspecting
our internal economy. Unfortunately, we
were striking camp, and the whole thing
collapsing, they retired. (It was arranged
by G. that they should come to tea, but
at the usual hour for that meal we had
just finished breakfast.)

32

Bone caves of the Wye.

Discovery of mysterious lump of limestone
Supposed bone of fossilus equis or fossil horse.

In the afternoon we explored the fields and met a young farmer engaged in harvesting who led us to his farm through apple orchards alive with geese and turkeys. He was very hospitable and we sat in his garden and drank cyder and talked through the afternoon. His family (butterfly catching) came round to the tent, which the ladies had already inspected during our absence and had remarked that they 'thought a woman might have made the place look more comfortable'.

Farmer welcomes us and sends for cyder.

A most worthy host, his cousins, sister and Aunts took much interest in our camp life and approached the tent with a view to inspecting our internal economy. Unfortunately, we were striking camp and the whole thing collapsing, they retired. (It was arranged by G that they should come to tea, but at the usual hour for that meal we had just finished breakfast.)

Bare caves of the Wye.

Discovery of mysterious lump of limestone, supposed bone of Fossilus equis or fossil horse

Bathing at Little Doward.

"Playing [sic] on the ole Banjo"

33

Hawk's skull found on L. Howard
(Astur palumbarius.)

At the 'King's Head'. Monmouth

Bathing at Little Doward.

Playing (sic) on the ole banjo.

We were striking tent and after adieus dropped down to Monmouth, laying up to have a broken rowlock mended, and we replenished our ale jars at an Inn. The keeper in attendance had spent a time in Edinburgh and was therefore accustomed to medical students, but fixed upon B. who is a layman as to the disciple of the healing art, much flattered that two men spent the afternoon and much tin there, and was found by the party still liquidating on their return from a tour of the place. All being now safely aboard we pushed off and rowed to Bigsweir where the tide is first felt, B. & Gg. landing to tow as far as Tintern.

Hawk's skull found at L. Doward (Aster palumbarius).

At the King's Head, Monmouth.

Tintern Abbey.

35

B. left the boat above Tintern and got last
in a wood. Afterwards found himself in
hotel and after devious wanderings
saw boat on other side the River.

Tintern Abbey

B. left the boat above Tintern and got lost in a wood. Afterwards found himself in hotel and after devious wanderings saw the boat on the other side.

Camp, 9 intern. As usual G. is putting up Tent. which
with other things was unloaded after much floundering.
in mud. Tide falling about a foot in 5 minutes

36

Effect of landing
in the mud.
Tintern

"Language"
from
farmer
at
Tintern
G. comes
in and
reports
farmer drunk.

Observe G's shocked expression.

After coming across to fetch B. we were all soon busy staggering through mud and water unloading the boat. It is a very rapid tide (at Chepstow the fall is about 40 feet) and our boat was soon left in the sludge and reeds while G. as usual, having first planted the standard, got the tent up and the baggage was transferred to its welcome cover, the canvas steaming from the heat of the lamp.

Camp Tintern. As usual G is putting up tent, which with other things was unloaded after much floundering in mud. Tide falling about a foot in 5 minutes.

Under such circumstances tea is the thing. We were imbibing some when a frightful hullabaloo proceeded from a farm somewhere near, and G. shouting in reply came in with the information that the farmer must be drunk as he could get no information to show what was wrong. We were too fagged to bother about it and went to sleep.

Effect of landing in the mud at Tintern

'Language' from farmer at Tintern. G. comes in and reports farmer drunk.

Observe G's shocked expression.

Farmer apologizes next morning, and sends
dark eyed daughter for cyder.

He says the girl will wash our things
and he will supply us with anything
we want.

We avail ourselves of the farmer's hospitality

One of the crew tries to ingratiate himself
with lovely maid by a present of
cornflour, onions and rice.

We paid a duty visit in the morning and the farmer finding we were customers, apologised, became affable and suggested his favourite ration, cyder, a handsome girl, his dark eyed daughter, bringing out a large jug of the same. He accentuated his remarks by a constant use of his forefinger and would have the girl wash our travel stained clothes if necessary. We soon enjoyed a much-needed ablution, and came away with eggs, milk and vegetables.

Farmer apologises next morning and sends dark eyed daughter for cyder.

He says the girl will wash our things and he will supply us with anything we want.

We avail ourselves of the farmer's hospitality

One of the crew tries to ingratiate himself with the lovely maid
by a present of cornflour, onions and rice.

Tintern Abbey. Interior.

Farmer's daughter
brings down a baby
to the great
confusion of the party.

Retirement of same.

Our artist has
the effrontery
to call this a
"Portrait
of
Goffe"

It was raining all day and we explored the abbey – a majestic pile. Yankees of course in evidence. G. & B. lunched at an Inn and afterwards trained to Chepstow, finding more Americans, H. & Gg. meanwhile occupying themselves in making a pudding of all the cornflour, eggs, custard powders etc. etc. in stock, proudly presenting same to the others on their return. It was voted 'off' and was made the medium of another interview with the dark eyed daughter and duly presented to her with a quantity of rice. She thought it would benefit the geese and seemed quite charmed with the gift. B. had been to the village for stores and had purchased some whiskey (for medicinal purposes). Calling at the farm on his return the farmer showed him silver prizes won at shows and the girl brought the inevitable cyder, an attention responded to by the production of the whiskey which the farmer seemed to much appreciate; the mixture however had a somnolent effect on B. who disgusted the party by snoring unbearably, until roused by boots and other moveable articles.

Breakfast next day was ready by 12 and dinner by 10 pm as we had got into most irregular habits; eggshells, unwashed articles thrown down anywhere and a general disinclination to amend had now settled down on the whole party. On Camping trips some order is necessary, and each man should take it in turn to set things in order, without which comfort is not

Tintern Abbey. Interior.

possible. Of course, away from houses one is apt to be somewhat careless in this respect, but here, close to the village, mixing with people, the contrast was most striking, the Hotel people of course thinking our habits a kind of outrage on the locus standi of the place, when every other building is a place of accommodation for tourists. One landlord quite 'gave us up' apparently thinking we were neither 'feather, flesh nor good red herring', but we drank his liquids and retired to our inexpensive if lowly couches fuelling that noble sense of independence dear to every British soul. 'Never was a more beautiful building erected on a more charming site than Tintern – it was founded by Cistercian monks in the early part of the 12th century by Waiter de Clare, its history uneventful, but very brief, for in 1537 it was given up into the hands of Henry VIII's Ecclesiastical commissioners and soon afterwards fell into ruins.'

'It is built of old red sandstone, cruciform in shape, the extraordinary beauty of the proportions and the extreme delicacy of the work must strike even the most casual visitor, and the impression is heightened by the exquisite bits of landscape of the surrounding hills that are framed within the empty mullions of the windows.' Length 228 ft. breadth 37 ft. transept 150 ft., height 70 ft. At back of N. transept are the conventional buildings.

Farmer's daughter brings down a baby to the great confusion of the party. Retirement of same.

Our artist has the effrontery to call this a 'Portrait of Goffe'.

Salmon fishing

H. was understood to say he would prepare breakfast
on our asking for it later, he indicated a mug
a milk can and a loaf lying on the grass!

To such dire straits may a camping party be
reduced after 'roughing it' for some time

As B. has to go to Glasgow he climbs a
bank to catch train at Chepstow

Salmon fishing.

H. was understood to say he would prepare breakfast. On our asking for it, he indicated a mug, a milk can and a loaf lying on the grass! To such dire straits may a camping party be reduced after 'roughing it' for some time.

As B. has to go to Glasgow, he climbs a bank to catch the
train to Chepstow

Broiling sun down mouth of River.
Exhaustion of G. and Gig
photo by H.

Brunel's Bridge Chepstow

At Chepstow Station. Messrs H. Gg & G.
have to take tickets, and produce in bring 2½
a fly-book, and such like valuable effects
It was suggested that H. do leave his gold watch
with an uncle residing in the town; he did not see
it. Station master eventually issues tickets,
keeping their luggage as security

We packed up and rowed down to Chepstow passing men salmon fishing, stone quarries on the left and soon the Iron Tubular Bridge of Brunel, 600 ft. long, divided into one span of 300ft. and three shorter spans of 100ft. each was passed.

The river widened considerably, the shores at low water looking desolate and generally unsuitable for camping. The castle at Chepstow is a mighty mass of masonry occupying nearly 4 acres on a platform of rock rising sheer from the river. It was originally built for one of the Norman Earls of Hereford in the 11th century, and is now in the possession of the Duke of Somerset who owns more ruined castles than any individual in Great Britain. The most stirring event in its history took place in the Civil Wars, and the fortress was taken by assault by Colonel Morgan after a short siege, many of the garrison with their brave commander being cruelly murdered. Henry Martyn the regicide was here imprisoned, as also for a short time a far better man – Jeremy Taylor. Here B. having to go North took a regretful leave. The rest of the crew dropped down to the mouth of the river, came back with the tide and pitched camp near Chepstow.

Broiling sun down the mouth of the river. Exhaustion of G. and Gg.

Brunel's Bridge, Chepstow

At Chepstow Station Messrs. H. Gg. and G. have to take tickets, and produced in bronze 2½, a fly-book and such like valuable effects. Station master eventually issues tickets, keeping their baggage as security.

At the last camp, Chepstow. Waiting for cart to
take baggage to
the station
H. photo.

The crew being photographed. U. C. Hospital
The End.

The boat was left at the landing stage in charge of Jordan's men and the remains of the stores handed over to some cottagers. A cart having been procured, the baggage was taken to the station-a little difficulty as to tickets was surmounted by leaving it in charge of the station master and the party took the train for town to once more undergo the regularity of every-day life and to look back on the contrasts afforded thereto by the incidents connected with 'Camping on the Wye'.

'The life is rough, but these things recommend themselves to those who, as Kinglake says: "not being born with chiffney bits in their mouths, are tired of living in a state of utter respectability, cruelly pinioned at dinner tables, or solemnly planted in pews".
'In the Forests of Brazil'
An Oxford Undergraduate

At the last camp, Chepstow, waiting for cart to take baggage to the station.

The crew being photographed. U. C Hospital

The end.

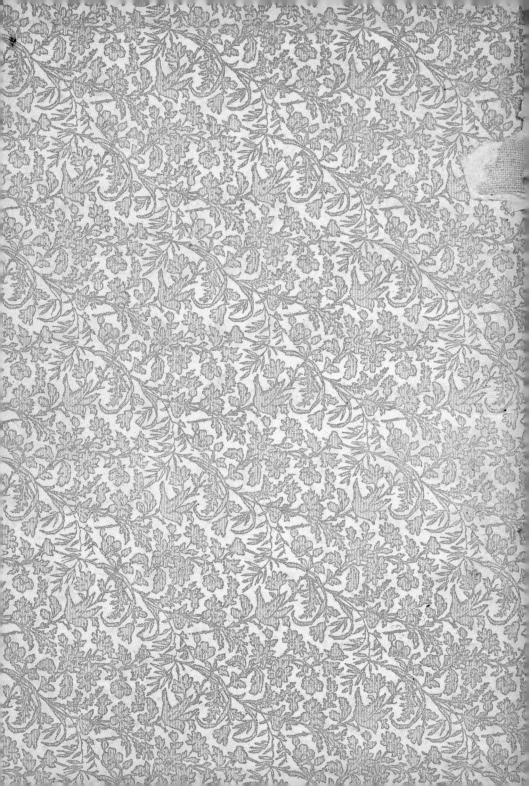